N.

The Delaplaine
2015 Long Weekend Guide

Andrew Delaplaine

NO BUSINESS HAS PAID A SINGLE PENNY OR GIVEN *ANYTHING* TO BE INCLUDED IN THIS BOOK.

A list of the author's other travel guides, as well as his political thrillers and titles for children, can be found at the end of this book.

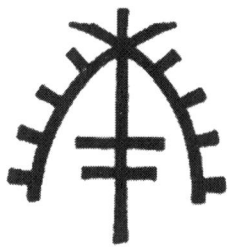

Senior Editors - *Renee & Sophie Delaplaine*
Senior Writer - **James Cubby**

Gramercy Park Press

Copyright © by Gramercy Park Press - All rights reserved.
Certain content licensed by Creative Commons per this link:
http://en.wikipedia.org/wiki/Founders%27_Copyright

Please submit corrections, additions or comments to
andrewdelaplaine@mac.com

NAPA VALLEY
The Delaplaine
2015 Long Weekend Guide

TABLES OF CONTENTS

WHY NAPA VALLEY? – 5

GETTING ABOUT – 9

WHERE TO STAY – 13

WHERE TO EAT – 27

WHERE TO SHOP – 47

COOKING CLASSES – 53

ATTRACTIONS – 57

WINERIES – 68

NIGHTLIFE – 79

SPAS – 80

INDEX – 84

OTHER BOOKS BY THE AUTHOR – 87

LONG WEEKEND SERIES

Like you, when I'm heading into a new place, I have bought travel guides and toiled through them hour after hour trying to extract from the book the "essence" of the city or region I was visiting. Sometimes, sadly, I spent more hours reading the book than I did in the town it purported to tell me about. To judge by the size of some of these books, you'd think I was planning on spending my life there, not just a few days.

By including exhaustive detail in their guidebooks, many writers actually end up obscuring the essence of the city they're writing about rather than revealing it.

If you're going to stay two or more weeks in a place, then by all means do your homework. There are hundreds of guides, both in print and online, to assist you.

But if you've only got 3 or 4 days, your needs really are different.

I would want to know:

= **LODGINGS**. What would be the best hotels or B&Bs or inns to choose from? I would want a choice of 4 or 5 places in different budget categories. (For the kid with a backpack will be on a different budget than someone on an expense account. A retired couple will have different wants and needs than a family of four.)

= **RESTAURANTS**. What would be a good selection of restaurants, again within different budget levels, that would represent the area I'm visiting? Again, whether expensive or cheap, which of the thousands of places to eat will give me a feel for the town?

= **ATTRACTIONS.** Of all the attractions and things to do, which are the most important that will leave me with memories that I've really *seen* the place?

= **SHOPPING?** Something different and out of the way reflective of the area. Not the big chains, whether that chain is Tiffany or the Gap. Something local.

Rather than craft a definitive itinerary for you the way many others have done, I've expanded the listings in each section so that you could get a good range of the offerings available—so you can pick and choose among them to craft your own special Long Weekend.

WHY NAPA VALLEY?

Depending on the time of year, there's nothing more fun than taking a trip out to the wine country, especially Napa and Sonoma counties. In fact, after you make your first trip, you'll come back and focus on this special part of America, so completely a world unto itself that there's literally nothing else like it in this country. I am in the wine trade myself (my family produces a fine sparkling wine using grapes from Napa and Sonoma), so I know a little bit about it.

The two valleys are just an hour's drive north of San Francisco.

The two counties are quite different in layout and attitude. Though Napa is more famous than Sonoma, winemaking actually began in Sonoma (in 1835) a whole generation before vineyards were planted in the 35-mile long Napa Valley. And while vineyards line Napa from one end to the other, in Sonoma there still are fields where vineyards have not been planted.

While Napa is narrow and more confined, in Sonoma, the land extends out from the Russian River far and wide, giving you a much more expansive sensation. Between Napa and Sonoma, there are hundreds of wineries large and small. Napa has some 45,000 acres planted with grapes. While Napa has all the celebrities, the high-end restaurants, the luxurious spas, Sonoma really feels like a rustic farming area by comparison. Much less razzmatazz. The good thing about both valleys is that they're right next to each other, so it's easy to enjoy both. But here our focus is on Napa.

Wine lovers didn't really begin flocking to this area until the 1980s, and the lodgings at the time were limited to a few inns and some B&Bs.

These days, however, you'll find superior lodgings to match anywhere in the world, complementing the high quality of the wines produced here.

Nobody thinks of this, but did you know there's a **Veterans Home** in Yountville? Now, I ask you, if you had been in the military, wouldn't you want to retire here?

GETTING ABOUT

Most people come to Napa by way of San Francisco, and the town of Napa itself is only 55 miles from San Francisco. The towns strung along the Valley moving north are: Napa, Yountville, Oakville, Rutherford, St. Helena and Calistoga. Sonoma County is just a few miles to the east of Napa Valley.

The Valley is only 35 miles from one end to the other, so (traffic permitting) it only takes a half hour to go from Napa in the south to Calistoga in the north on Hwy. 29 (also known as the St. Helena Hwy.).

The **Silverado Trail**, some 2 miles away, run parallel to Hwy. 29, and during peak traffic, makes a faster alternative if you're in a hurry. Also has splendid views.

High season runs from March through the harvest in October, and this is when the place is jammed with tourists. I heartily advise people making their second trip to come in those fringe areas of the off-season, early March or early November, let's say, to get a sense of what it's like to really live here. Deals are more easily had in the off-season, of course, and you end up spending more time with the locals than you (or they) have time for in the crush of summer.

The drunk driving laws are very severe in California, and they are firmly enforced. Even if you drive up, unless you have a dedicated driver, it sometimes is a good idea to hire a driver. These drivers also act as tour guides, so you're getting a lot more than the ride.

BUS SERVICE
There is a bus service called **The Vine** running up and down the Valley that's easy to use.
http://www.ridethevine.com/

HIRE A DRIVER

ST. HELENA WINE TOURS
www.shwinetours.com/

Fleet has Jaguar sedans, vans for larger parties, stretch limos and Lincoln Navigators. Rates from $60/hour. (Ken Slavens is often recommended if you want to ask for someone specific.) Wide range of wine tours. They'll also do "dinner runs" if you want a taxi service. Check for rates.

PERATA LUXURY TOURS
707-227-8271
www.perataluxurycarservices.com/
Personalized wine tours, dinner trips, airport service, and just about anything else you want. From $68 per hour, with minimum hourly requirements. They use Chevy Suburbans.

VISITOR INFORMATION

Napa Valley Conference & Visitors Center
1310 Napa Town Center, Napa: 707-226-7459
www.napavalley.com
Comprehensive information on lodgings, restaurants, spas, activities while you're there, wineries. (They have a winery map you can just print out a copy on their web site).

WHERE TO STAY

AIRBNB.COM
www.airbnb.com

Definitely look into the scourge of hoteliers everywhere in the world, this site that alerts frugal travelers to bargain lodgings in people's homes almost anywhere in the world. You might find a flat a block from Champs Élysées that's a third of the price of a small room at the Georges V and with a lot more charm.

Voilà!

You will need to do your research, but the good thing is that you pay Airbnb.com directly, not the person hosting you.

They get protections from you (if you're a crazy person and trash the host's apartment, you will pay dearly) and you get protection from them (in case they offer something not available in the rental).

All in all, a wonderful meeting of the minds for savvy travelers looking for bargains and people in cities where travelers want to go who want to maximize the revenue potential of that spare room.

I have several friends of mine who do this in Miami, on South Beach where I live, and they are all happy with the entire experience.

ARBOR GUEST HOUSE
1436 G St., Napa: 707-252-8144
arborguesthouse.com
This B&B has 3 suites in the main house and 2 suites in the Carriage House. This timeless estate features an enchanting gazebo and tranquil sitting areas throughout the garden where guests can relax their minds and forget the rush of everyday life, play a mellow game of bocce ball or stroll the beautifully cultivated grounds. Retire to the living room for afternoon wine with nosh or relax and read the paper by the fire.

ANDAZ NAPA
1450 First St., Napa: 707-687-1234
http://napa.andaz.hyatt.com
Right in downtown Napa, the Andaz makes an excellent choice if you want to explore the 14 tasting rooms in the immediate area featuring some of the best wines in California. All the usual amenities. (A Hyatt property.)

AUBERGE DU SOLEIL RESORT
180 Rutherford Hill Rd., Rutherford: 707-963-1211
aubergedusoleil.com
Since 1985, this has been a top place to stay. They have a collection of sun- and earth-toned rooms and suites, each featuring French doors opening onto private terraces, cozy fireplaces and sensuous elements such as private soaking tubs for two. For the Auberge's signature style of soft-spoken luxury, the partners tapped renowned designer Michael Taylor, who infused his dramatic California style with the essence of Provence. Full spa services. (Try the milk chocolate bath in-suite, for a touch of decadence.) Certainly one of Napa's most luxurious resorts, with one of the area's best restaurants, the **Bistro & Bar**.

Since it's really pricey, check out the Bistro first. Here you can order a couple of small plates to taste (from $6) and get a glass of wine (from $9), and not break the budget while taking advantage of the sunset on the terrace or the fire crackling inside.

BARDESSONO
6526 Yount St., Yountville: 707-204-6000
www.bardessono.com/spa/
They have 62 rooms in downtown Yountville. Each is designed for in-room spa services. The menu in the restaurant here is based on local, farm-fresh ingredients. A real treat is the rooftop pool where you can also dine. I've been all over the world, but I've never seen a menu item reading "freshly dug carrot salad." I'm tempted to write that it's "so freshly dug you can still taste the dirt on the carrot," but I'm not. (In any case, go for the parsnip soup—it's really good.) They have a wide selection of fish here, and it's painstakingly prepared, but don't overlook the lamb T-bone: you almost never see that cut (it's served with fennel, squash and "saffron spaetzle," and it's excellent).

BEAZLEY HOUSE
1910 First St., Napa: 707-257-1649
beazleyhouse.com
"Napa's first & still its finest bed & breakfast nn." Or so they say. It really is a nice place, a beautifully converted old house. Jim and Carol Beazley set up shop in 1981. You stay in rooms in either the Mansion or the Carriage House (opened in 1983), which has 5 rooms, each with its own entrance, fireplace, 2-person tub. The Beazley House is just a short walk from the newly revitalized downtown Napa riverfront, the Opera House, the Wine Train, fine dining, shopping, and Napa's Oxbow Market.

Dog friendly, free Internet access, tasty breakfasts made in-house, lovely gardens. And they're always sprucing up the place.

CALISTOGA RANCH
580 Lommel Rd., Calistoga: 855-942-4220
www.calistogaranch.com/
The "lodges" here offer private patios, fireplaces, great views of the 150+ acre compound. Oak groves abound, so you're really quite in the country. Very posh. Yoga deck. Expensive, of course, starting from $900. Very private, facilities and grounds top-notch. (Take a look into their wine cave. Kind of eerie.)

CANDLELIGHT INN
1045 Easum Dr., Napa: 707-257-3717
candlelightinn.com
Candlelight Inn — a luxurious Napa Valley B&B. Located near downtown Napa, this lovely 1929 English Tudor inn is centrally located to all the wonders of wine country, yet oh, so far away. Situated on an acre of land beneath towering redwood trees along the banks of the Napa Creek, this place feels like a park. A romantic and restful backyard, manicured gardens and a gorgeous swimming pool.

CARNEROS INN
4048 Sonoma Hwy., Napa: 707-299-4900
http://www.thecarnerosinn.com
You can see for miles from the vantage point of the rise where the inn is situated. There are almost no trees obstructing the view, which gives the place a rather Spartan feel, but it's quite luxurious. Great lodgings, restaurant and bar. Open and airy, lots of windows.

CEDAR GABLES INN
486 Coombs St., Napa: 707-224-7969
cedargablesinn.com
A luxurious 10,000 square foot mansion made into a B&B. They offer a 3-course gourmet breakfast, evening hors d'oeuvres and wine tasting. It's all quite grand for a B&B, but you won't argue.
Napa Cooking Classes
Paired with outstanding wines from the best wine producing region in the world, the Cedar Gables Inn Cooking School offers the ultimate Napa Culinary Experience: Hands on cooking classes with top notch chefs from the area. Following the class you get to eat what you made in the Inn's elegant dining room.

CHELSEA GARDEN INN
1443 Second St., Calistoga: 707-942-0948
chelseagardeninn.com
Set among lush garden paths, Chelsea Garden Inn has one-bedroom suites with private entrances, private

baths and fireplaces. Has a seasonal pool, jasmine-lined walkways, whimsical touches, bold colors, fine linens, down pillows, and other amenities in every private suite.

GOLDEN HAVEN HOT SPRINGS SPA AND RESORT
1713 Lake St., Calistoga: 707-942-8000
goldenhaven.com
Calistoga hot springs water and rejuvenating spa treatments. After a day of touring Napa Valley, you can swim in their hot springs pool, relax on the sun deck, plop into a mud bath and otherwise perk up with their Calistoga spa treatments.

HENNESSEY HOUSE
1727 Main St., Napa: 707-226-3774
hennesseyhouse.com
Downtown Napa just a stroll away from this wonderful Queen Anne style house built in the 1890s. (The porch was added in 1901.) Eggs Florentine for breakfast. Fireplaces, two-person whirlpool tubs and featherbeds in some rooms. The place is stuffed with great antiques. Very comfy.

HOTEL YOUNTVILLE
6462 Washington St., Yountville: 707-967-7900
www.hotelyountville.com/
You don't even need a car when you get here. So many great places to eat are within walking distance, you could spend a week here and never get in a car. Lots of little boutiques for shopping, and 4 wine tasting rooms nearby. Their concierge will help you navigate the Napa area if you want them to. Free bikes. Let them know what you're interested in before you arrive and they'll map out what you need to do to see it all. **Spa AcQua** is located here. They have 6 treatment rooms, 2 couple's "spa suites" featuring Vichy showers, luxurious double hydrotherapy tubs and fireplaces. Decadent? Oh, yes. Check out their web site to see the kind of specially priced packages they offer that might apply to you when you travel. (Especially good off-season.)

INDIAN SPRINGS
1712 Lincoln Ave., Calistoga: 707-942-4913
indianspringscalistoga.com
Lovely palm tree-lined drive takes you to this historic spa resort at the northern end of the Napa Valley. California's oldest continuously operating pool and spa facility. Situated on 16 acres planted with olive and palm trees, roses and lavender, the property has 4 thermal geysers that produce an extraordinary supply of rich mineral water. Another prized asset is the vast, natural deposit of pure volcanic ash on the acreage.

INN ON RANDOLPH
411 Randolph St., Napa: 707-257-2886
innonrandolph.com
Located in heart of downtown Napa, it's only a short walk to over a dozen tasting rooms, popular restaurants, evening activities and local events.

LAVENDER
2020 Webber Ave., Yountville: 800-522-4140
lavendernapa.com
What they've achieved here is a combination of modern luxuries and top-notch services and given it all the look and feel of a B&B. "Conde Nast Traveler" voted it one the "Top 50 Small Hotels," and that's no accident. An old house forms the center of complex of 4 buildings. There's a wraparound porch, an enclosed verandah where breakfast is served. They've made every effort to give you the feeling you're in Provence. (And they come damn close.)

MAISON FLEURIE
6529 Yount St., Yountville: 800-788-0369
www.maisonfleurienapa.com
Charming (and not too costly) B&B in ivy-covered stone buildings dating back to the 1870s. Better than average breakfast. Wine and canapés in the late afternoon. Lovely gardens.

MEADOWOOD
900 Meadowood Lane, St. Helena: 800-458-8080
www.meadowood.com
Luxurious resort in a splendid country setting. They do everything here: weddings, sporting events (they have a pool, tennis courts, golf), conferences, events and a wide variety of seasonal offerings (like a Thanksgiving special that's very nice). It's one thing to see how "the other half" live, but here you can see how they relax.

From $650 to over $1,000 per night. (If you're a foodie, you'll want to know that **The Restaurant at Meadowood** got 3 stars from Michelin.)

THE NAPA INN
1137 Warren St., Napa: 707.257.1444
napainn.com
14 rooms and suites are individually decorated. Each has private bathroom and fireplace. Some have two-person whirlpool tubs and all have showers. The Napa Inn observes Eco-friendly practices. A gourmet candlelight breakfast is served each morning in the Napa Inn dining room or on the garden patio. Evening wine and refreshments.

OLD WORLD INN
1301 Jefferson St., Napa: 707-257-0112
oldworldinn.com
As one of Napa's first bed and breakfasts, the Old World Inn is known for two things: home-style food and friendliness. You get freshly baked chocolate chip cookies when you check in. At 5:30, hey have a little wine reception. You get chocolate desserts when you return to the Inn each evening. Two-course breakfast is served.

PETIT LOGIS
6527 Yount St., Yountville: 877-944-2332
www.petitlogis.com/
Completely seductive inn with only 5 rooms. It's not a B&B in the sense that there's no breakfast. (But there's the famous **Bouchon Bakery** just next door where you can get a REALLY great morning snack!

They open at 7 a.m., by the way.) The rooms here, while comfy and rustic (they even have fireplaces), still offer completely updated amenities: big bathrooms, Jacuzzi tubs, refrigerators, wireless Internet. Great restaurants like the **French Laundry** are just down the street.

VILLAGIO INN & SPA
6481 Washington St., Yountville: 707-944-8877
villagio.com
Located on the 23-acre Vintage Estate, Villagio Inn & Spa has been dubbed by "Town & Country" Magazine as a "pleasure seeker's heaven." This Tuscan-inspired Yountville hotel property features flowing water fountain pathways weaved throughout lush Mediterranean-style gardens. The San Francisco Chronicle Magazine described their rooms and suites as "massive, terribly tasteful and terribly elegant." You'll agree. This is a much larger place than most lodgings you find in the area. Free bottle of white wine when you arrive. Charming, with balconies, porches, fireplaces, Jacuzzi in your room.

WHERE TO EAT

ANGELE
540 Main St., Napa: 707-252-8115
angelerestaurant.com
CUISINE: French
DRINKS: Full Bar
SERVING: Lunch / Dinner
Has a menu that layers elements from traditional recipes with contemporary influences. Its focus on rich and soothing French cuisine ranges from the classic simplicity of fresh, seasonal salads to the robust balance of bœuf bourguignon. Whether seated at a table in the dining room, at the full bar or outside on the terrace overlooking the Napa River, enjoy

lunch and dinner surrounded by a simple, family-style setting.

BISTRO DON GIOVANNI
4110 Howard Ln., Napa: 707-224-3300
bistrodongiovanni.com
CUISINE: Italian
DRINKS: Full Bar
SERVING: Lunch/ Dinner
The best tasting meals are prepared simply, and with the freshest ingredients. They source their herbs, vegetables and produce from local farmers and support ranches that raise humanely-treated, free-roaming livestock and poultry. All of the menu items are inspired by the bounty of the region and prepared with utmost attention to detail. Donna's way of selecting and combining seasonal products to highlight pure, robust flavors in an ever changing

variety has drawn a steady stream of loyal diners. Great wine list, of course.

BISTRO SABOR
1126 First St., Napa: 707-252-0555
bistrosabor.com
CUISINE: Latin American
DRINKS: beer & wine
SERVING: lunch & dinner (except closed Sunday and Monday)
Here you'll get the kind of street food you only find in Latin America. Really delicious ceviches (Peruvian style), *posole* (a Mexican stew) and *pupusas* (thin tortilla filled snacks from El Salvador). Every Saturday night from 10 to 1, things get busy with Salsa, Merengue, Cumbia, Bachata and Reggaeton. You're invited to DANCE! No cover charge.

CELADON
500 Main St., Napa: 707-254-9690
celadonnapa.com

CUISINE: International; seafood
DRINKS: Full Bar
SERVING: Lunch/ Dinner
Enjoy Celadon's award-winning 'Global Comfort Food' in their beautiful dining room or out in the lovely courtyard. The seasonally influenced menu features flavors from the Mediterranean, Asia, and the Americas.

LA TOQUE
1314 McKinstry St., Napa: 707-257-5157
latoque.com
CUISINE: American; French
DRINKS: Full Bar
SERVING: Dinner
The menu evolves constantly to show off each season's finest ingredients. They have developed a network of local farmers and purveyors who supply

them with some of the finest foods in the world. The Options menu is presented in three sections from which you can create your own multi-course experience. Their Chef's Tasting Menu and Vegetable Tasting Menu are presented in a fixed format of five courses.

MUSTARDS GRILL
7399 Saint Helena Hwy., Napa: 707-944-2424
www.mustardsgrill.com/
CUISINE: American
DRINKS: Full bar
SERVING: Lunch, Dinner
No class distinctions here. You'll find local cops and firefighters plopping down for this excellent food, sitting right next to famous celebrities, including Bobby Flay, who said the Mongolian pork chop he ate here was one of the best dishes he ever ate.

OENOTRI
1425 First St., Napa: 707-252-1022
oenotri.com
CUISINE: Italian
DRINKS: Full Bar
SERVING: Lunch/ Dinner
Oenotri is an Italian restaurant in downtown Napa featuring a daily changing menu driven by ingredients that are local, fresh and in season. They celebrate culinary traditions rarely seen elsewhere in California — the specialties of Sicily, Campania, Calabria, Basilicata and Puglia. Salumi is handcrafted in house,

and their pasta is made fresh daily, and ALL their pasta selection are standouts. As part of their goal to serve quality artisanal pizza, they imported a wood-fueled Acino oven from Naples to bake authentic pizza Napoletana.

PEARL
1339 Pearl St., Napa: 707-224-9161
therestaurantpearl.com
CUISINE: American
DRINKS: Beer/ Wine
SERVING: Lunch/ Dinner
Pearl is a casual bistro just off the main streets of downtown Napa. Owners Nickie and Peter Zeller have created an energetic and exciting space with soaring ceilings, vibrant local artwork and comfortable seating both indoors and on the front patio. As its namesake suggests, Pearl starts by offering oysters, raw on the half shell, or roasted with salsa verde and feta. Other starters include soft tacos with ginger marinated flank steak and house made tortillas, crab cakes and Guerrero style corn on the cob with chili cream, cojita cheese and lime. A variety of sandwiches served on house focaccia, soft polenta with sauteed seasonal vegetables and roasted tomato sauce, daily fish specials, Jose's chicken verde. Get the triple double frenched pork chop with apple brine. Dessert: a seasonal fruit crisp, johnnycake cobbler, pineapple upside down cake, or a variety of house made sorbets and ice creams.

PRESS
587 St. Helena Hwy., St. Helena: 707-967-0550

www.presssthelena.com/
CUISINE: Steakhouse
DRINKS: Full bar
SERVING: Dinner
While the steaks are the big draw here, get one of their rotisserie chickens and cut it up to share. Extensive collection of wines. Impeccable service.

THE THOMAS
813 Main St., Napa: 707-226-7821
www.thethomas-napa.com/
CUISINE: American, Live, Raw Food
DRINKS: Full bar
SERVING: Dinner, Brunch
This place is steeped in mystery as there was a murder here in the early '70s, but now it's been redone as an adorable three-level eatery and bar. The food is "seasonal California" and worth the trip. Awesome view on the balcony.

VINTNER'S COLLECTIVE TASTING ROOM
1245 Main St., Napa: 707-255-7150
www.**vintnerscollective**.com
Another great spot for tasting the wines of many different wineries, all under the roof of an historic building that has been restored. The building has an interesting history all its own: it formerly housed a brothel, a brewery, a laundry, a meat company and a saloon.

ZUZU
829 Main St., Napa: 707-224-8555
zuzunapa.com
CUISINE: Spanish Tapas
DRINKS: Beer/ Wine
SERVING: Lunch/ Dinner/ Weekends dinner only
The restaurant offers a modern, California version of tapas along with some traditional offerings based on the cuisines of Spain, Portugal and the Mediterranean. The Chefs of ZuZu are inspired by fresh, seasonal ingredients and places an emphasis on using organic and sustainable produce, seafood and meats.

YOUNTVILLE

A little over 50 miles north of San Francisco. Less than 3,000 people call this place "home." You wouldn't think so in the summer, which is why it's a great place to visit off-season. Great deals not only in the restaurants, but in area lodgings as well. There are 6 Michelin stars in little Yountville, and they are all within a few blocks of each other.

AD HOC
6476 Washington St., Yountville: 707-944-2487
www.adhocrestaurant.com/
CUISINE: American
DRINKS: Full bar
SERVING: Dinner, Sunday brunch

One of premier Chef **Thomas Keller's** establishments, this one is quite informal, down to the point that there's only one brief, 4-course menu each night. But worry not, the same exacting standards regarding ingredients are employed here as in his other, more formal, eateries. The menu changes nightly, features family-style cuisine, If you're lucky, the night you're there they'll have the chicken fricassee or the buttermilk fried chicken or the "pork 'n pickles" (baby back ribs, sweet potato mostarda with lots of pickles to cut the fat. Oh, my!
ADDENDUM is the small take-out shack behind Ad Hoc (closed in winter; opens in April) where you can pick up boxed lunches of fried chicken or their great BBQ for $16 Thursday through Saturday; closed Sunday-Wednesday; 707-944-1565.

BOTTEGA RISTORANTE
6525 Washington St., Yountville: 707-945-1050
www.botteganapavalley.com/
CUISINE: Italian
DRINKS: Full bar
SERVING: Lunch, Dinner
Owner Michael Chiarello works the room like a Broadway star. (Get a table facing the kitchen; they have the best view of the room.) The standout here is the gnocchi.

BOUCHON BAKERY
6528 Washington St., Yountville: 707-944-2253
bouchonbakery.com/
CUISINE: French bakery
DRINKS: no booze

SERVING: 7 a.m. to 7 p.m.
All foodies know that this bakery is owned by the famed **Thomas Keller**, owner of the **French Laundry**. Come here for baked goods prepared using the classic recipes: pastries, Viennoiserie, cookies, macaroons. But also for breakfast, confections, quiche (the ham quiche for breakfast is a standout), sandwiches, salads, picnic baskets, even treats for your pets.

FRENCH LAUNDRY
6640 Washington St. (at Creek St.), Yountville: 707-944-2380
www.frenchlaundry.com
CUISINE: American; French; Michelin rated
DRINKS: beer & wine
SERVING: lunch Friday-Sunday 11-1; dinner nightly

from 5:30; DRESS CODE: don't even think about jeans or shorts or slovenly dress; men ought to bring a jacket, even a tie if you want to fit in.

Get ready for the meal of your life. All professional foodies know about this very expensive Thomas Keller eatery located in a wonderful setting in the wine country. Reserve as far ahead as you can, because it's murder to get in. But once you do, you'll be treated to one of the best dining experiences of your life. You do tend to get the feeling you're in church when you're here, so reverent are the diners and so focused are the staff. But just surrender to Keller's prix-fixe menu of 9 courses. You'll be amused at the tiny portions (you don't exactly need a microscope to see them), but they all add up to a very filling meal by the time you finish. And, much more important, an experience you'll *never* forget. When Keller dies, people will weep. $270.

REDD
6480 Washington St., Yountville: 707-944-2222
www.reddnapavalley.com/
CUISINE: International (they call it "wine country cuisine," but it's got things from Europe, Asia and America); Michelin rated.
DRINKS: full bar
SERVING: lunch, brunch, dinner (call ahead, it's tough getting in)

I'm partial to the smoked trout at lunch as well as the caramelized scallops with a cauliflower purée. (If they have it when you're there, get the chestnut soup.) If you go for brunch, get the Hangtown omelet with fried oysters and pancetta. The crispy chicken thigh is great. The pork tenderloin with bacon and butternut squash will have you rolling your eyes. They have a "bacon-infused" Bloody Mary that offers a super twist on what you'd expect. Chef Richard Reddington cut his teeth working at Masa's and Jardiniere in San Francisco.

REDD WOOD
6755 Washington St., Yountville: 707-299-5030
www.redd-wood.com
CUISINE: Pizza, American
DRINKS: Full bar
SERVING: Lunch, Dinner
The décor looks like it's just a lot of old junk, but that mailbox over there used to stand in front of Robert Mondavi's house. And yes, it's pizza, but it's pizza by a Michelin starred chef named Richard Reddington.

ST. HELENA

CINDY'S BACKSTREET KITCHEN
1327 Railroad Ave., St. Helena: 707-963-1200

www.cindysbackstreetkitchen.com/
CUISINE: American / Mexican
DRINKS: Full bar
SERVING: Lunch, Dinner
One of Cindy Pawlcyn's eateries. (Others are **Mustards Grill** and **Wood Grill & Wine Bar**). It's really American with some Mexican inspiration using authentic quality ingredients. Comfortable atmosphere with warm, unpretentious service.

GILLWOODS CAFÉ
1313 Main St., St. Helena: 707-963-1788
www.gillwoodscafe.com/
CUISINE: Breakfast & Lunch Diner
DRINKS: Beer & Wine
SERVING: Breakfast, Lunch

A local favorite serving the best breakfast in town. Good variety of sandwiches for lunch. Prompt service.

GRILL AT MEADOWOOD
900 Meadowood Lane, St. Helena: 707-968-3144
www.meadowood.com/
CUISINE: American
DRINKS: Wine
SERVING: Breakfast, Lunch, Dinner
Not as gussied up as the more formal restaurant, the Grill overlooks the golf course and is much more casual. Weekend brunch is a must here. Daily menu with ingredients fresh from the Meadowood garden.

GOTT'S ROADSIDE TRAY GOURMET
(formerly Taylor's)
933 Main St., St. Helena: 707-963-3486
www.gotts.com/

CUISINE: Burgers, Diner
DRINKS: Beer & Wine
SERVING: Breakfast, Lunch, Dinner
Don't let the "fast food joint" look of this place put you off. It serves some of the finest quality food to be found around here, and locals flock to it.

THE RESTAURANT AT MEADOWOOD
900 Meadowood Lane, St. Helena: 702-967-1205
www.meadowood.com

Black truffle gnocchi with parsnip Mousse and brown butter, king salmon with beets, Pacific black cod with white asparagus, chanterelles, bonito. There's also a smoked chicken that's unusual. (3 stars from Michelin.)

CALISTOGA RESTAURANTS

ALL SEASONS BISTRO
1400 Lincoln Ave., Calistoga: 707-942-9111
allseasonsnapavalley.net
CUISINE: American
DRINKS: Beer/ Wine
SERVING: Lunch/ Dinner
Smoked baby back ribs, braised lamb shank with crispy shallots, smoked ribeye. Opened This was among the first restaurants in the United States to receive the Wine Spectator's prestigious "Grand Award." Seasonal and regional ingredients, sustainable farming and fishing, small production, handcrafted wines.

BAROLO
1457 Lincoln Ave., Calistoga: 707-942-9900
barolocalistoga.com
CUISINE: American/ Italian
DRINKS: Full Bar
SERVING: Dinner
Witty sophistication meets rustic hip with Barolo's unique mix of simple food done simply well, coupled with an unpretentious and approachable local wine list. Great music and a cool, laid-back vibe are a hallmark of this popular Calistoga eatery known for its great food and friendly service.

BOSKO'S TRATTORIA
1364 Lincoln Ave., Calistoga: 707-942-9088
boskos.com
CUISINE: Italian/ Pizza

DRINKS: Beer/ Wine
SERVING: Lunch/ Dinner
Italian comfort food, simple Italian classics, large servings at reasonable prices.

SOLBAR
In **Solage Resort**
755 Silverado Tr., Calistoga: 877-684-6146
solagecalistoga.com
CUISINE: American
DRINKS: Full Bar
SERVING: Breakfast/ Lunch/Dinner
Try the Maitake mushroom pizza here. This place is your best option in these parts for great pizza, and it's the only pizza available on the Silverado Trail. The dough at Solbar is based upon a biga-style starter, which cultivates and propagates the yeasts, developing a more complex flavor within the crust. Traditionally, Italian bakers use a biga starter for making ciabatta bread, and Solbar's pizza crust definitely features some ciabatta-like characteristics.

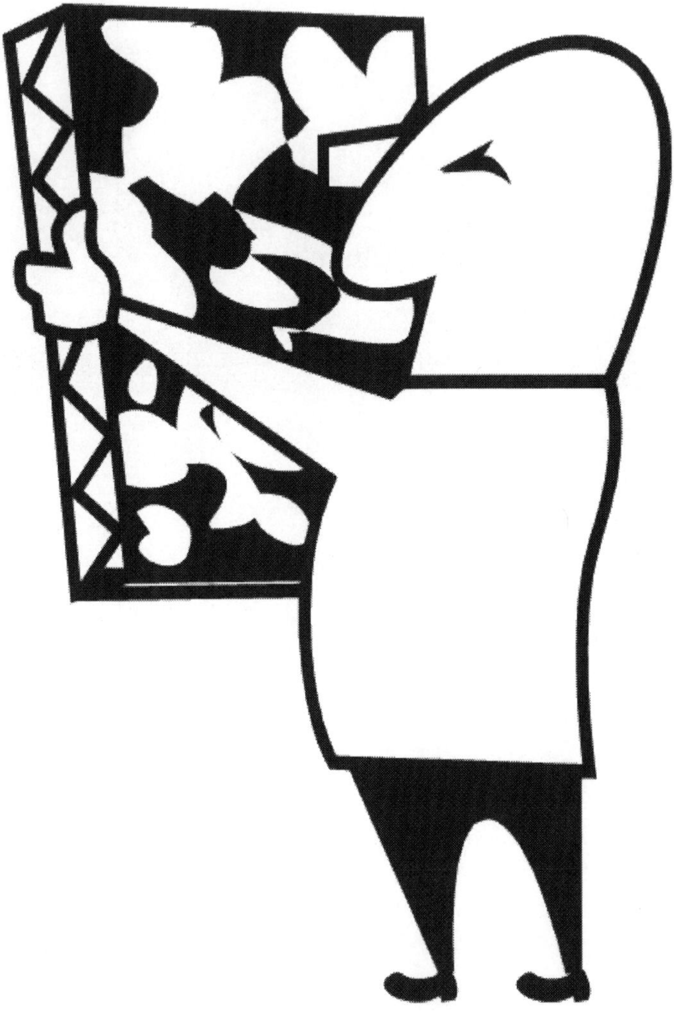

WHERE TO SHOP

BACK ROOM WINES
1000 Main St., Suite 100, Napa: 707-226-1378
backroomwines.com/
Great series of wine tastings and other wine-related events. Perfect store to buy wine to take back home.

DEAN AND DELUCA
607 St. Helena Hwy., St. Helena: 707-967-9980
www.deandeluca.com
You've always had it in your mind that you'd have a picnic in the idyllic wine country, right? Here's where you pick out the things that'll go in the basket. Great gifts.

FOOT CANDY
1239 Main St., St. Helena: 707-963-2040
www.footcandyshoes.com/
For women who love shoes, and what woman doesn't? An amazing selection of designer names like Christian Louboutin, Jimmy Choo and Manolo Blahnik.

MA(I)SONRY
6711 Washington St., Yountville: 707-944-0889
maisonry.com/

There are only 3 stone buildings in Yountville, and this 1904 structure built as a private house or manor is one of them. Inside, you'll find a wide array of furnishings—some old, some new, and some representing some of today's top designers. They also have wine tastings ($10 and up) that include a carefully selected list, including owner Michael

Polenske's **Blackbird Vineyards** wines which closely mirror Pomerol. Beautiful gardens in the back. Don't forget to go upstairs. You'll find a lot of surprises there, including costumes (oil on paper) painted by Ralph Lauren's nephew, Greg Lauren.

NAPA VALLEY COFFEE ROASTING COMPANY
1400 Oak Ave., St. Helena: 707-963-4491
www.napavalleycoffee.com/
The best coffee possible. Made-to-order espresso drinks and freshly brewed coffee, pastries and cookies. Custom roasts bagged to go.

NAPASTYLE
6525 Washington St., Yountville: 707-945-1229

www.napastyle.com/
If you ever want someone to whip up a picnic basket, get this place to do it. But the big draw here is housewares and gourmet delicacies.

Great wines and unusual gifts like Maldonado Servers, Vintage Milk Canisters and Vintage Spoon & Fork Pendant Lights.

NAPA VALLEY OLIVE OIL MANUFACTURING COMPANY

8325 Charter Oak Ave., St. Helena: 707-963-4173
www.oliveoilsainthelena.com
The Particelli family grows the olives in the Sacramento Valley that makes the oil they sell here in their store. The bottles holding the extra virgin and infused oils are filled one-by-one by hand.

STEVE'S HARDWARE & HOUSEWARES
1370 Main St., St. Helena: 707-963-3423
www.acehardware.com
Your local Ace Hardware for all of your hardware and household needs.

WOODHOUSE CHOCOLATE
1367 Main St., St. Helena: 707-963-8413
www.woodhousechocolate.com/
Chocolates, they're special here. Luscious, delectable handmade chocolates.

COOKING CLASSES

CASA LANA B&B
1316 S. Oak St., Calistoga: 877-968-2665
www.casalana.com
Casa Lana offers "Gourmet Retreats" for home cooks and food enthusiasts. The hands-on classes are taught in the B&B's professionally equipped kitchen and range in length from a 5-hour class to a full 5-day

Culinary Learning Vacation. The small class size (up to 8 people) provides personalized attention for each participant. Private classes and Team Building sessions are also available.

THE CULINARY INSTITUTE OF AMERICA AT GREYSTONE
2555 Main St., Helena: 707-967-1100
http://enthusiasts.ciachef.edu/boot-camps
One- and Two-Day Programs. Invigorating Mornings in the Kitchen. You'll don chef's whites and head right into the kitchen for lecture, hands-on cooking, and food and wine pairings. There's no shortage of fascinating topics to explore, from the cuisines of Northern California to healthy sustainable eating and live-fire grilling.

You'll enjoy lecture, hands-on cooking, and a wine tasting and sensory analysis session, and come away with a better understanding of the flavors of California.
Tuition varies for 1 and 2-day programs.

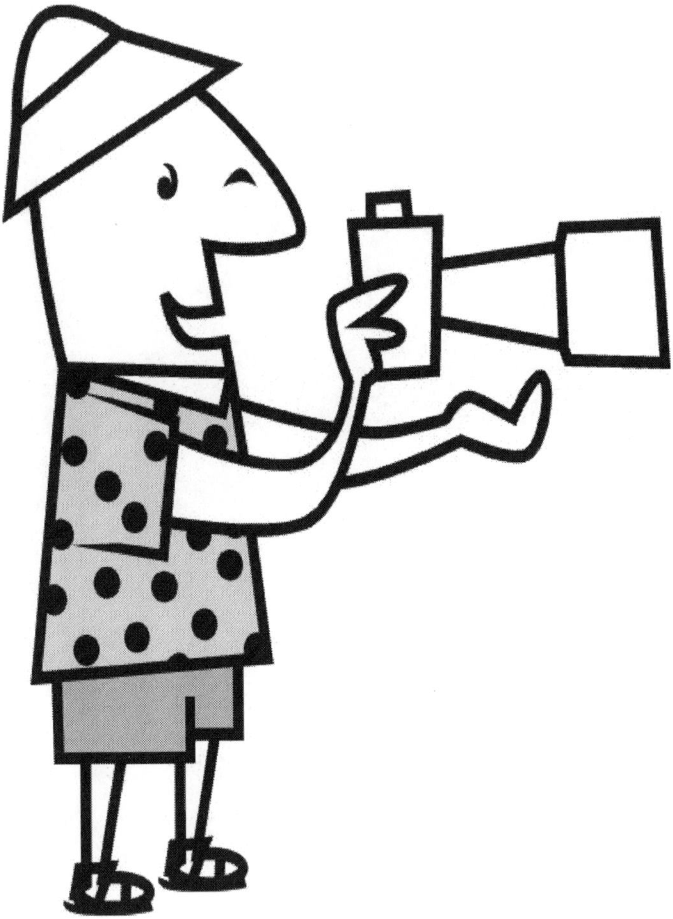

ATTRACTIONS

ART WALK
www.townofyountville.com
This is a collection of three dozen sculptures that run up and down the street downtown.

BEAU WINE TOURS
1680 Pear Tree Ln., Napa: 707-257-0887
beauwinetours.com
Looking for something a little more economical than your own private limo?
Interested in meeting other people and making friends on a fun Daily Tour?

Daily wine tour in the Napa Valley. Full day of wine tasting. Each tour starts with free champagne served on-board one of their cars or buses. The guide takes you to four boutique wineries. Includes a picnic lunch from the Girl & the Fig Restaurant, served at one of the many hidden-gem locations in the valley (usually among vineyard views, garden terraces or wine cellars depending on weather). Lunches are served "family style" allowing everyone to pick and choose from a variety of sandwiches, side salads, and desserts. Fees apply.

CALISTOGA FARMER'S MARKET
1235 Washington St., Calistoga: 707-942-8892
calistogafarmersmarket.org
Saturdays, 8:30 a.m. - 12 Noon; May 7 through October 29. Sharpsteen Plaza located across from the City Hall in downtown Calistoga.

CASTELLO DI AMOROSA
4045 St. Helena Hwy., Calistoga: 707-967-6272
www.**castellodiamorosa**.com
A crazy winemaker, **Dario Sattui,** for all his life in love with medieval architecture, built this fantastic castle of over 100 rooms (I think I remember that it has over 120,000 square feet), all in the style of the ancient castle-fortresses of Northern Italy. An $18 admission fee gives you not only a tour of the place, but also a tasting of 5 of their wines. There's a Knight's Room featuring frescoes, a torture chamber, a chapel (actually used for weddings and whatnot), extensive wine cellars—all of it will give you a feeling that you're FAR away from the Napa Valley.

CRANE PARK
360 Crane Avenue, St. Helena: 707-967-2792
city.ci.st-helena.ca.us/section.cfm?id=75
They offer nightly bocce here that's popular with locals. As Francis Ford Coppola said, "There are 138 local teams and it's really fun. We like bocce because you can play holding the ball in one hand and a glass of wine in the other." 10 acre park with 6 lighted tennis courts, 4 lighted bocce ball courts, 2 Little League baseball fields, horse shoe pits, children's play ground and individual and group picnic areas. Also site of **St. Helena Farmers Market**, open from 7:30 to 11:30 a.m. every Friday, May through October.

GOURMET NAPA WALKING TOUR
415-312-1119
COST: $68 per person
gourmetwalks.com
There is more to Napa than just wine tasting. Welcome to the FIRST culinary walking tour in Wine Country, for those who know that California cuisine is just as sought after as its wine. Tour covers downtown Napa. Get the fascinating history of this riverfront town, one where celebrity chefs intermingle with organic farmers and boutique winemakers. You start at the **Oxbow Market**, where there's a seasonal bounty of California specialty foods and produce. Tour crosses the Napa River to visit 19th century historic buildings that weathered Prohibition to showcase the latest trends in California food and

wine. You'll leave the tour with a carefully curated list of Wine Country restaurant recommendations and recipes for your next meal. NOTE: Customers must be over 21 and bring valid ID to participate in wine tastings.

NAPA RIVER ADVENTURES GUIDED RIVER BOAT CRUISES
816 Third St., Napa: 707-224 9080
COST: varies by age.
www.napavalleyadventuretours.com
Their captains give an incredibly in-depth, insider tour of the Napa River and everything that is connected to it. All cruises are aboard the ElectraCraft electric boat, which comfortably seats up to 11 passengers. Seating is limousine-style and the wrap-around windows provide panoramic views from every seat. Guests are encouraged to bring beverages and snacks. Begins with a narrative of the Napa River and the impact it has had on the local community. As you head north along the Napa River passing through the recently restored wetlands and head towards historic downtown Napa, you will be able to see remnants of the past and understand how present changes will affect the future of Napa. Sweeping vistas of the valley. You will note the change in the temperature, wind along the cruise, and understand the unique micro-climates that enable Napa Valley to produce exceptional wines. Tides and times permitting, they will also pass Copia: The American Center for Wine, Food and Art, and the Napa Yacht Club.

NAPA DOWNTOWN FARMERS' MARKET
500 First St., Napa: 707.501.3087
www.napafarmersmarket.com
The Napa Certified Farmers Market has been bringing fresh, local produce, specialty foods and artisan crafts to the City of Napa, California, for more than 20 years. Tuesdays and Saturdays from 7:30 a.m. until noon

NAPA VALLEY BALLOONS
One California Drive, Yountville: 707-944-0228
COST: $240 per person, add $10 for in-flight photo
napavalleyballoons.com
Voted "Best Balloon Ride" 1996-2010. Featured on the Today Show, Oprah and the Travel Channel. The company trusted to fly Chelsea Clinton. Pre-flight & post-flight breakfast and champagne. Comfortable state-of-the-art aircraft. They've been flying hot air balloons over the Napa Valley for about 30 years.

They have FAA certified pilots and aircraft, a professional staff and an impeccable safety.

NAPA VALLEY BIKE TOURS
6795 Washington St., Bldg. B, Yountville: 707-944-2953
COST: Fees vary depending on package. Rates start at $89 per person.
napavalleybiketours.com
Full-service bike tour company since 1987. They offer single-day guided winery tours by bike, self-guided winery tours by bike and bike rentals, as well as custom Napa Valley vacation packages.

NAPA VALLEY OPERA HOUSE
1030 Main St., Napa: 707.226.7372
nvoh.org
Napa Valley Opera House is the jewel of the Valley that showcases excellence in music and performing arts for audiences of all ages including world-class

musical theatre, plays, chamber music, jazz, opera, dance and family programs. In a place where the nightlife is, shall we say, limited, you'd do well to see what's playing when you're in the area.

NAPA VALLEY WINE TRAIN
1275 McKinstry St., Napa: 800-427-4124
COST: Varies upon lunch/ dinner and car chosen to ride in
winetrain.com
The tracks upon which the Napa Valley Wine Train runs were originally built in the 1860s to bring guests to the hot spring resort town of Calistoga. While the track to Calistoga no longer exists, much of the rest of the route is unchanged. Due to the immense influence that rail transport had over the development of the communities and wineries of the Napa Valley, there is no shortage of sights to see during the 3-hour journey to St. Helena. Five towns; Napa, Yountville, Oakville, Rutherford, and St. Helena; and numerous

wineries can be seen through the large picture windows on board the Wine Train.

VISTA DOME - Intimate, special and above the crowd. Almost 180-degree Napa Valley vistas under the antique dome windows. Enjoy wine pairing events and romantic moonlight dinners.

GOURMET EXPRESS - Relive the luxury and tradition of railroad dining as the steward seats you in the Gourmet car. White linen service for half your journey. The other? The comfort of the lounge car.

SILVERADO - Taste the barbeque side of Napa Valley gourmet in the Silverado car. This open-air railcar has a relaxed atmosphere, with a western theme and sliding windows.

Take the Ferry from San Francisco. Getting here from San Francisco could not be easier - or more pleasant. Hop on a ferry and enjoy a Bay cruise on your way to the Wine Train.

You must make reservations at least a day in advance.

The San Francisco-Napa Connection is available only with their lunch trains. Reservations required. Leave San Francisco at 8:30, be back by 7. Depending on the time of year, you might take the Ferry or the Bus. Check the "Mode of Transportation Table" for details. Both the Ferry and the Bus will drop you off in Vallejo where you will board the Napa Valley Wine Train Shuttle.

SAFARI WEST
3115 Porter Creek Rd., Santa Rosa: 707-579-2551
COST: Varies by season.
safariwest.com

Here in the heart of California's wine country... in the field of wheat-colored grass, on the slopes of rolling green hills, among the trees and ranches and vineyards is where you will find the essence and spirit of Africa. Not a zoo...not a drive through park...this is the home of Nancy and Peter Lang. A captivating tapestry of raw sounds and earthy smells; a magic place with the sights and sounds of the Serengeti where the air is filled with melodious chirps from the aviary, squawking calls from gregarious parrots, and a occasional lemur screech. An African style oasis where guests experience a rare sense of freedom and gain renewed inspiration. Enjoy all the creature comforts when you spend the night in one of their luxury tents—"It's like having a tent over your room." Pale-green canvas walls enclose plush beds, hot showers and rustic but elegant trappings. There are polished wood floors, custom wood-slab countertops in the private bathrooms and one-of-a kind hand hewn furniture. There is nothing more magical than falling asleep to the sounds of a kookaburra and waking to the resounding love-songs of the sarus cranes. Removed from televisions, computer screens and even cell-phone reception, gazing over the rolling hills and roaming herds from your private tent deck is the ultimate in high-definition viewing.

SILO'S MUSIC ROOM
530 Main St., Napa: 707-251-5833
COST: Cover charges depends on entertainment
silosnapa.com

Premier Music Room and Wine Bar features the best in live Rock, Motown, Reggae, and Jazz alongside Napa's finest wines and draft beers. Conveniently located right in Downtown Napa at the Historic Napa Mill and Napa River Inn. Open Wednesday through Saturdays.

ST. HELENA'S FARMERS' MARKET
Crane Park St., Helena: 707-486-2662
sthelenafarmersmkt.org
Fridays, 7:30 a.m. till Noon; May through October. Rain or Shine. Located in Crane Park, just south of town behind the St. Helena High School.

WINE COUNTRY BUS TOURS
415-353-5310
COST: varies by age.
www.supersightseeing.com
Napa and Sonoma are world famous for their fine wine and beautiful scenery. Learn about wine from their expert guides as you travel north to the wine country. You'll learn the history of winemaking, from the early Spanish missionaries who brought grape vines from Europe to the Forty-Niners who served wines in their saloons. You will tour wineries and see how grapes are picked, crushed, blended and bottled. You'll walk through beautiful vineyards with your tour guide and then taste the finished product – wine-tasting fees included. There will be time for lunch at Historical Sonoma Square or Vintage 1870 in the heart of Napa. ALL TOURS include pick-up and drop-off at most San Francisco Hotels. Approx. 9 hours. Departs: 9 a.m.

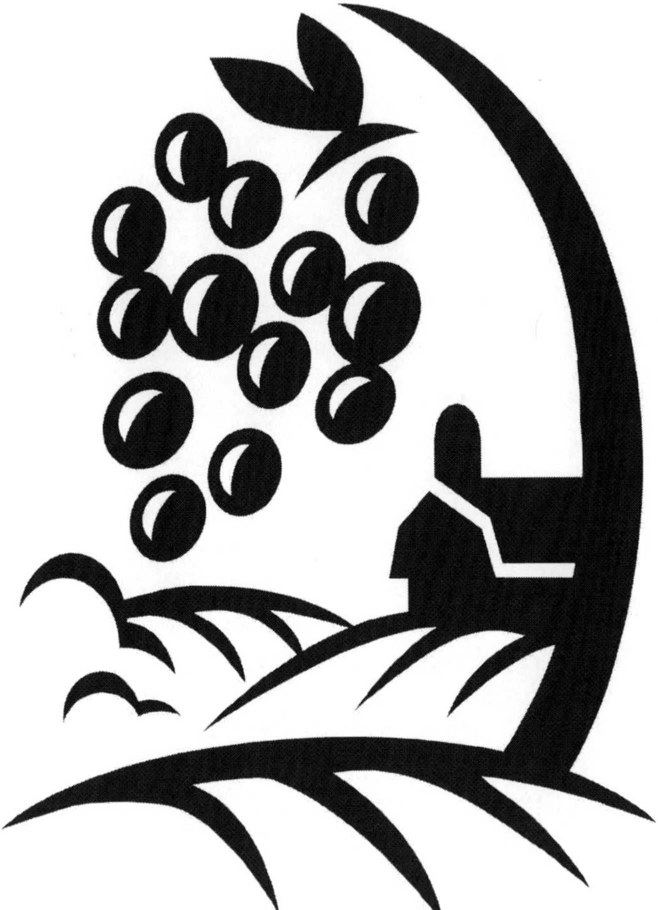

WINERIES

There are over 300 wineries in the region, but I'm not going to give you anything like a comprehensive list. Here are the ones I'd choose from if I had a limited amount of time to spend in the Valley.

DARIOUSH
4240 Silverado Trail, Napa: 707-257-2345
www.darioush.com/
Darioush Khaledi, a passionate wine man, started this place in 1997 and even in that short time he has built an exceptional winery. He grew up in the Shiraz region of Iran, and left after the revolution.

DOMAINE CHANDON
1 California Dr., Yountville: 707-944-2280
www.chandon.com

An excellent spot to stop for a tasting and to experience the first-class job they do here. The Möet et Chandon people launched this winery in 1973 to produce American sparkling wine at affordable prices and in the same manner they make it in France, what's called "method champenoise." You'll love the gardens and art.

FRANK FAMILY VINEYARDS
1091 Larkmead Lane, Calistoga: 707-942-0859
www.frankfamilyvineyards.com/

Their wines are really popular all over L.A. because Rich Frank's sons Paul and Darryl are how biz execs (Paul is executive producer of *Royal Pains*, and Darryl is prexy of DreamWorks TV). Frank himself was formerly president of Walt Disney Studios, so you can see why Hollywood types flock here. Has a wine club with over 2,000 members. While they're noted for their high-priced Cabs, the Frank family Napa Valley Cabernet Sauvignon sells for under $50.

HALL RUTHERFORD
56 Auberge Rd., Rutherford: 707-967-0700
COST: $40 per person
hallwines.com/hall-rutherford
Hall Rutherford is Craig and Kathryn Hall's stunning winery amid the legendary Sacrashe vineyard. Completed in March of 2005, this high-tech facility has been carefully designed for the production of small-lot red wine. Custom made three-to-six-ton fermenters afford their winemakers great flexibility

and precision handling of vineyard blocks and the ability to micro-manage every aspect of the winemaking process. Unlike the Halls' St. Helena property, which is able to handle more significant quantities of grapes during harvest, this compact gravity-flow winery is dedicated solely to the production of rare and single vineyard red wines. The winery's 14,000 square feet of caves were designed and built by Friedrich Gruber of Gutenstein, Austria. The caves are finished with handmade Austrian brick recovered from sites in and around Vienna. The caves showcase select works from the Halls' art collection. Deep inside the caves is a reception area for private tastings and entertaining. The room's chandelier, designed by Donald Lipski and Jonquil LeMaster, is dressed in hundreds of Swarovski crystals.

HALL WINES
401 St. Helena Hwy., St. Helena: 707-967-2626
www.hallwines.com/
Founded in 1885, noted for its classic Bordeaux varietals. Daily tours & tastings.
tour and barrel tasting offers a first hand look into the life of a wine, from barrel to bottle.

INGLENOOK WINERY
1991 St. Helena Hwy., Rutherford: 707-968-1100
www.inglenook.com/
A lot of people don't know this, but famed "Godfather" director Francis Ford Coppola, in addition to his eponymous winery in the Sonoma Valley, also owns this fabled winery. It sits on 1,600 acres of prime Napa Valley vineyard land. It's been

producing highly valued cabs since the 1940s. The filmmaker bought this winery in 2011 after it had fallen into disrepute as a maker of cheap wines. He now lives in a house at this winery and his plans call for Inglenook to regain its former cachet.

JOSEPH PHELPS VINEYARDS
200 Taplin Rd., St. Helena: 707-963-2745
www.josephphelps.com
Phelps was in the construction business back in the '60s when he first came here (to build a winery, actually). Like a lot of other people, he fell in love with the Valley, but he did something more than dream about it. He bought some vineyards and went into a new career. This is not a place where you will see busloads of bedraggled tourists pouring into a tasting room. Here you'll need an appointment. They have several different tastings available. A beautiful winery, famous for its reds.

KENZO ESTATE
3200 Monticello Rd., Napa: 707-254-7572
www.kenzoestate.com/
Kenzo Tsujimoto bought 3,800 acres here in 1990 and had sedulously worked to put together a team that makes wines served in some of the best spots in the U.S. The first vintage, 2005, was all sent back to Japan. All the great Bordeaux varietals are represented (and some Sauvignon Blanc.)

RAVENA
2930 St. Helena Hwy., St. Helena: 707-967-8814
www.revanawine.com/
Cabernet Sauvignon is the name of the game here. You have to get an appointment, but well worth the trouble. Small, family owned producer of world-class wines.

ROBERT MONDAVI WINERY
7801 St. Helena Hwy., Oakville: 707-226-1395
www.robertmondaviwinery.com/

Located in the heart of Napa Valley, the Robert Mondavi Winery is part of the To Kalon vineyard. The First Growth Vineyard produces some of the most notable and award-winning Cabernet and Fume Blanc wines in the world. Mondavi was one of the first wineries to offer tours, tastings, culinary and art programs.

RAYMOND VINEYARDS
849 Zinfandel Lane, St. Helena: 707-963-3141
http://www.raymondvineyards.com
While other wineries have their "tasting rooms," the folks here at Raymond have gone all out to create a dizzying array of feel-good places for you to experience their wines. They have the Crystal Room, the Barrel Room, the Library, the Theatre of Nature, the Rutherford Room and the Corridor of Senses. In

the Crystal Room, for example, they have a collection of old decanters you have to see. A crystal chandelier (by Baccarat) hangs above you. You're flanked by stainless steel walls and a mirrored bar. In the Red Room club (membership is $500 for a year, and you can bring up to 3 guests), you can slip into a private lounge where you can play billiards, drink wine, use a vintage pinball machine and enjoy the plushness of more red velvet than you ever thought you'd see.

SCHRAMSBERG VINEYARDS
1400 Schramsberg Rd., Calistoga: 707-942-4558
www.schramsberg.com/

Producers of elegant vintage Pinot Noir and Chardonnay based sparkling wines in the traditional méthode champenoise. Tastings by appointment only. Tours (booked in advance) are 5 times a day.

SWANSON VINEYARDS
1271 Manley Lane, Rutherford: 707-754-4018
www.swansonvineyards.com/
This winery produces Merlot, Cabernet Sauvignon, Pinot Grigio and Dessert Wines from their Oakville vineyards. Two distinct tastings for wine lovers are offered (reservations required).

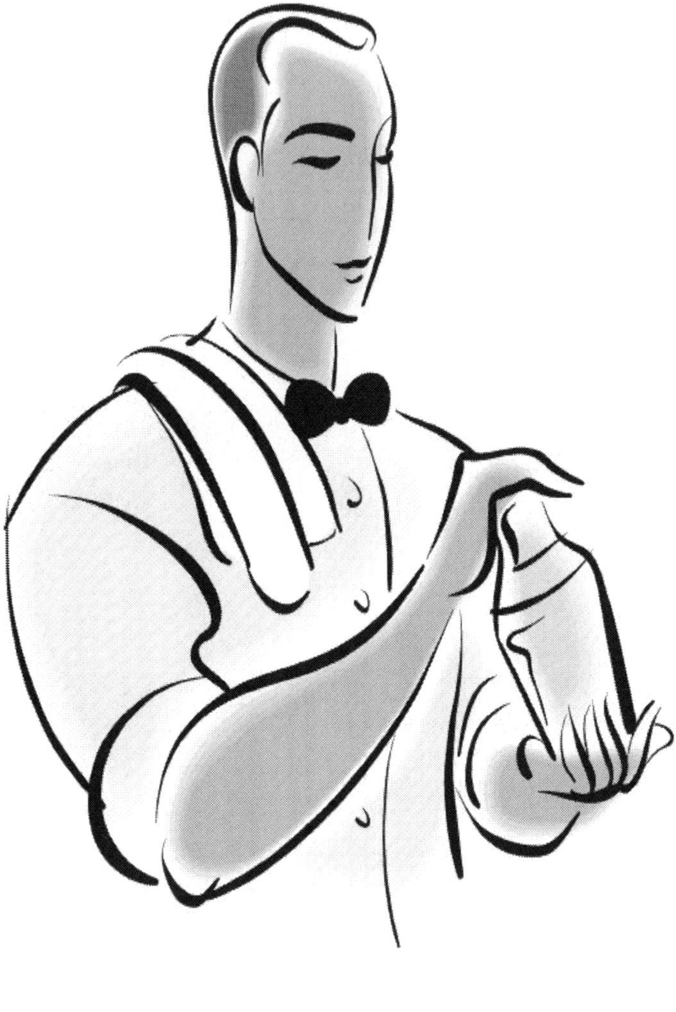

NIGHTLIFE

Nightlife here means dinner and drinking. If you're serious about nightlife, go back to San Francisco.

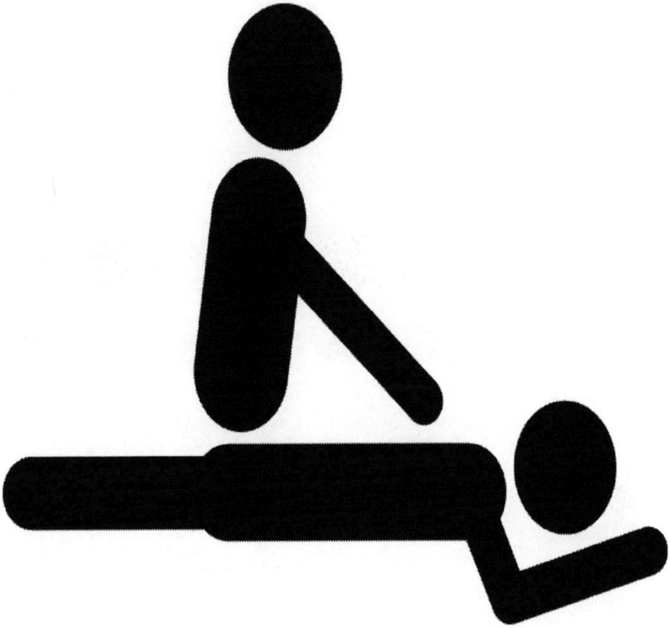

SPAS

CALISTOGA SPA HOT SPRINGS
1006 Washington St., Calistoga: 707-942-6269
calistogaspa.com
Facilities include separate Men's and Women's Spas, four outdoor Mineral Water Pools, Exercise and Aerobics rooms, and Conference Facilities seating forty.

EURO SPA & INN
1202 Pine St., Calistoga: 707.942.6829
eurospa.com
TripAdvisor Travelers' Choice Award Winner, 2010. Relaxing & intimate atmosphere, serene pool setting, neighboring vineyard views, true hospitality, downtown Calistoga location.

GOLDEN HAVEN HOT SPRINGS
1713 Lake St., Calistoga: 707-942-8000
goldenhaven.com
Calistoga Golden Haven Hot Springs Spa is nestled in the heart of California's Napa Valley wine country and makes the perfect Calistoga spa getaway. Come and experience the magic of the Calistoga hot springs water and rejuvenating spa treatments. After a day of touring Napa Valley, you can swim in
Their hot springs pool, relax on the sun deck under the California sun, and rejuvenate with our famous Calistoga spa treatments.

LAVENDER HILL SPA
1015 Foothill Blvd., Calistoga: 707.942.4495
lavenderhillspa.com
Just a few steps from the historic Napa Valley Wine Country town of Calistoga, elegantly seated in a terraced garden hillside, you will find tiny and tranquil Lavender Hill Spa. A harmonious blend of

Napa Valley Wine Country beauty with exotic Asian influenced statuary and art create the perfect setting for high quality Calistoga spa treatments.

MOUNT VIEW HOTEL & SPA
1457 Lincoln Ave., Calistoga: 707-942-6877
mountviewhotel.com
Voted Best Boutique Resort by Bohemian 2010. Cabanas, Pool, Jacuzzi, Day Spa, Breakfast in Bed, Winery Suites, WIFI and more.

SPA SOLAGE
755 Silverado Tr., Calistoga: 707-226-0806
solagecalistoga.com/spa/
Health and wellness are at the heart of the Solage experience. Artfully designed and ecologically conscious, Spa Solage offers relaxing and invigorating services, including new twists on the renowned Calistoga mud and mineral water therapies.

INDEX

A

AD HOC, 36
ADDENDUM, 37
AIRBNB.COM, 13
ALL SEASONS BISTRO, 44
American, 36, 44, 45
ANDAZ NAPA, 15
ANGELE, 27
ARBOR GUEST HOUSE, 14
ART WALK, 57
AUBERGE DU SOLEIL RESORT, 15

B

BACK ROOM WINES, 47
BARDESSONO, 16
BAROLO, 44
BEAU WINE TOURS, 57
BEAZLEY HOUSE, 17
Bistro & Bar, 15
BISTRO DON GIOVANNI, 28
BISTRO SABOR, 29
Blackbird Vineyards, 49
BOSKO'S TRATTORIA, 44
BOTTEGA RISTORANTE, 37
Bouchon Bakery, 24, 37
BUS SERVICE, 10

C

CALISTOGA FARMER'S MARKET, 58
CALISTOGA RANCH, 18
CALISTOGA SPA HOT SPRINGS, 81
CANDLELIGHT INN, 18
CARNEROS INN, 18
CASA LANA B&B, 53
CEDAR GABLES INN, 19
CELADON, 29
CHELSEA GARDEN INN, 19
CRANE PARK, 59

D

DARIOUSH, 69
DEAN AND DELUCA, 47
DOMAINE CHANDON, 69

E

EURO SPA & INN, 81

F

FOOT CANDY, 48
FRANK FAMILY VINEYARDS, 70
French Laundry, 25, 38

G

GILLWOODS CAFÉ, 41
GOLDEN HAVEN HOT SPRINGS, 82
GOLDEN HAVEN HOT SPRINGS SPA AND RESORT, 20

GOTT'S ROADSIDE TRAY GOURMET, 42
GOURMET NAPA WALKING TOUR, 60
GRILL AT MEADOWOOD, 42

H

HALL RUTHERFORD, 71
HALL WINES, 72
HENNESSEY HOUSE, 20
HOTEL YOUNTVILLE, 21

I

INDIAN SPRINGS, 22
INGLENOOK WINERY, 72
INN ON RANDOLPH, 22
Italian, 37, 44

J

JOSEPH PHELPS VINEYARDS, 73

K

Keller, Thomas, 37, 38
KENZO ESTATE, 74

L

LA TOQUE, 30
LAVENDER, 22
LAVENDER HILL SPA, 82

M

MA(I)SONRY, 48
MAISON FLEURIE, 23
MEADOWOOD, 23
MOUNT VIEW HOTEL & SPA, 83
MUSTARDS GRILL, 31, 41

N

NAPA DOWNTOWN FARMERS' MARKET, 62
NAPA INN, THE, 24
NAPA RIVER ADVENTURES' GUIDED RIVER BOAT CRUISES, 61
NAPA VALLEY BALLOONS, 62
NAPA VALLEY BIKE TOURS, 63
NAPA VALLEY COFFEE ROASTING COMPANY, 49
NAPA VALLEY OLIVE OIL MANUFACTURING COMPANY, 50
NAPA VALLEY OPERA HOUSE, 63
NAPASTYLE, 49

O

OENOTRI, 32
OLD WORLD INN, 24
Oxbow Market, 60

P

PEARL, 33

PERATA LUXURY TOURS, 11
PETIT LOGIS, 24
PIZZA, 44
PRESS, 33

R

RAVENA, 74
RAYMOND VINEYARDS, 75
REDD, 39
REDD WOOD, 40
Restaurant at Meadowood, 24, 43
ROBERT MONDAVI WINERY, 74

S

SAFARI WEST, 65
SCHRAMBERG VINEYARDS, 76
SILO'S MUSIC ROOM, 66
Silverado Trail, 9
SOLBAR, 45
Spa AcQua, 21
SPA SOLAGE, 83
SPANISH, 35
St. Helena Farmers Market, 59
ST. HELENA WINE TOURS, 10
ST. HELENA'S FARMERS' MARKET, 67

STEVE'S HARDWARE & HOUSEWARES, 51
SWANSON VINEYARDS, 77

T

THE CULINARY INSTITUTE OF AMERICA AT GREYSTONE, 54
THOMAS, THE, 34

V

Veterans Home, 7
VILLAGIO, 25
Vine, The, 10
VINTNER'S COLLECTIVE TASTING ROOM, 35

W

WINE COUNTRY BUS TOURS, 67
Wood Grill & Wine Bar, 41
WOODHOUSE CHOCOLATE, 51

Z

ZUZU, 35

Other Books by the Same Author

Andrew Delaplaine has written in widely varied fields: screenplays, novels (adult and juvenile), travel writing, journalism. His books are available in quality bookstores as well as all online retailers.

Jack Houston
St. Clair Political Thrillers
The Keystone File – Part 1
The Keystone File – Part 2
The Keystone File – Part 3
The Keystone File – Part 4
The Keystone File – Part 5
The Keystone File – Part 6
The Keystone File – Part 7 (final)

On Election night, as China and Russia mass soldiers on their common border in preparation for war, there's a tie in the Electoral College that forces the decision for

President into the House of Representatives as mandated by the Constitution. The incumbent Republican President, working through his Aide for Congressional Liaison, uses the Keystone File, which contains dirt on every member of Congress, to blackmail members into supporting the Republican candidate. The action runs from Election Night in November to Inauguration Day on January 20. Jack Houston St. Clair runs a small detective agency in Miami. His father is Florida Governor Sam Houston St. Clair, the Republican candidate. While he tries to help his dad win the election, Jack also gets hired to follow up on some suspicious wire transfers involving drug smugglers, leading him to a sunken narco-sub off Key West that has $65 million in cash in its hull.

THE RUNNING MATE
A Jack Houston St. Clair Political Thriller

Sam Houston St. Clair has been President for four long years and right now he's bogged down in a nasty fight to be re-elected. A Secret Service agent protecting the opposing candidate discovers that the candidate is sleeping with someone he shouldn't be, and tells his lifelong friend, the President's son Jack, this vital information so Jack can pass it on to help his father win the election. The candidate's wife has also found out about the clandestine affair and plots to kill the lover if her husband wins the election. Jack goes to Washington, and becomes involved in an international whirlpool of intrigue.

MARY FREEMAN SERIES
MIDNIGHT MASS - A Mary Freeman Thriller

Det. Lt. Mary Freeman stumbles upon a spectacular robbery of historic Trinity Church in downtown Manhattan on Christmas Eve, and after impressing the Mayor, gets assigned to the Task Force investigating the crime, throwing her headlong into a world of political intrigue and murder that rips apart every aspect of her life.

Jake Bricker Series

THE METER MAID MURDERS

A Jake Bricker Comic Thriller

A serial killer is loose on South Beach. But he's only killing meter maids, threatening the economic foundation of Miami Beach. Mayor Johnny Germane wants the killer caught NOW! But tall, dark and handsome Det. Sgt. Jake Bricker can't seem to nab the devious killer, even though he knows who the next victim will be. [Foul language; not for kids.]

The Adventures of Sherlock Holmes IV

In this series, the original Sherlock Holmes's great-great-great grandson solves crimes and mysteries in the present day, working out of the boutique hotel he owns on South Beach.

THE BORNHOLM DIAMOND

A mysterious Swedish nobleman requests a meeting to discuss a matter of such serious importance that it may threaten the line of succession in one of the oldest royal houses in Europe.

THE RED-HAIRED MAN

A man with a shock of red hair calls on Sherlock Holmes to solve the mystery of the Red-haired League.

THE CLEVER ONE

A former nun who, while still very devout, has renounced her vows so that she could "find a life, and possibly love, in the real world." She comes to Holmes in hopes that he can find out what happened to the man who promised to marry her, but mysteriously disappeared moments before their wedding.

THE COPPER BEECHES

A nanny reaches out to Sherlock Holmes seeking his advice on whether she should take a new position when her prospective employer has demanded that she cut her hair as part of the job.

THE MAN WITH THE TWISTED LIP

In what seems to be the case of a missing person, Sherlock Holmes navigates his way through a maze of perplexing clues that leads him through a sinister world to a surprising conclusion

THE DEVIL'S FOOT

Holmes's doctor orders him to take a short holiday in Key West, and while there, Holmes is called on to look into a case in which three people involved in a Santería ritual died with no explanation.

THE BOSCOMBE VALLEY MYSTERY

Sherlock Holmes and Watson are called to a remote area of Florida overlooking Lake Okeechobee to investigate a murder where all the evidence points to the victim's son as the killer. Holmes, however, is not so sure.

THE SIX NAPOLEONS

Inspector Lestrade calls on Holmes to help him figure out why a madman would go around Miami breaking into homes and businesses to destroy cheap busts of the French Emperor. It all seems very insignificant to Holmes—until, of course, a murder occurs.

The Trap Door Series

THE TRAP DOOR: THE "LOST" SCRIPT OF CARDENIO

A boy goes back to 1594 and Shakespeare's original Globe Theatre in search of a "lost" play by the world's greatest writer, and ends up embroiled in the plot to kill Queen Elizabeth the First and replace her with Mary, Queen of Scots. [Highly suitable for kids.]

The Annals Of Santopia

SANTOPIA: PART I, BOOK 1
SANTA & THE LOST PRINCESS

Three days before Christmas in the year 1900, Connie Claus has a son, and Santa names the boy Nicholas. Ameritus, Great Sage of Santopia, issues a Prophecy – the next girl born in the Kingdom will grow up to become Prince Nicky's Queen, and Nicky will become betrothed to her on his eighteenth birthday when he is invested as the future Santa at the Ritual of the Green Gloves. Far across Frozen Lake, the Baroness von Drear gives birth to a baby girl – she's overjoyed that her new baby will be the future Queen of Santopia. But when she discovers another girl was born just hours before her own to Taraxa and Inula, peasant family living in her Realm, she sets out to destroy them.

SANTOPIA: PART I, BOOK 2
SANTA & THE TRUTH REVEALED

It's Christmas Eve, and Elf Duncan journeys to the Other World as a stowaway on the Grand Sleigh. When discovered, he is forced to stay with the Red Elves in their Warren deep below the Tower of London until Santa can send a sleigh to bring him home. Back in Santopia during the same time period, Spicata rescues Taraxa and Inula from the carnivorous Pirandelves and gets them safely to Santopolis where he hopes to discover the real story behind the missing baby girl, thinking his reward would be great if he could get new information to the Baroness.

Screenplays

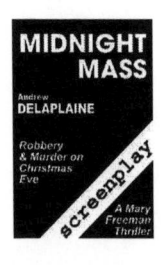

MIDNIGHT MASS – THE SCREENPLAY

Det. Lt. Mary Freeman stumbles upon a spectacular robbery of historic Trinity Church in downtown Manhattan on Christmas Eve, and after impressing the Mayor, gets assigned to the Task Force investigating the crime, throwing her headlong into a world of political intrigue and murder that rips apart every aspect of her life. (Based on the novel.)

MEETING SPENCER – THE SCREENPLAY

After a series of Hollywood flops, famed director Harris Chappell (Jeffrey Tambor in the movie released in 2012) returns to New York to relaunch his Broadway career. But Chappell's triumphant comeback begins to spiral out of control into a wild night of comic misadventure after meeting struggling actor Spencer (Jesse Plemons) and his old flame Didi (Melinda McGraw). This is an original script (not based on a novel or other source material). This is the original script, NOT the shooting script. You can stream the movie on Netflix. Or buy it on Amazon.

THE TRAP DOOR – THE SCREENPLAY

Looking for a famous "lost" play, a London boy performing in "A Midsummer Night's Dream" travels back in time to 1594 and the original production of the play in the original Globe Theatre. While there, he becomes embroiled in a plot to assassinate the Protestant Queen Elizabeth the First and replace her with the Catholic Mary, Queen of Scots. (Based on the novel.)

Delaplaine Travel Guides

Delaplaine Travel Guides represent the author's take on some of the many cities he's visited and many of which he has called home (for months or even years) during a lifetime of travel. The books are available as either ebooks or as printed books. Owing to the ease with which material can be uploaded, **both the printed and ebook editions** are updated 3 times a year.

The Long Weekend Series

Annapolis
Appalachicola
Atlanta
Austin
Berlin
Beverly Hills
Birmingham
Boston
Brooklyn
Cancún (Mexico)
Cannes
Cape Cod
Charleston
Charlotte
Chicago
Clearwater – St. Petersburg
Coral Gables
El Paso
Fort Lauderdale
Fort Myers & Sanibel
Gettysburg
Hamptons, The
Hilton Head
Hollywood – West Hollywood
Hood River (Ore.)
Jacksonville
Key West & the Florida Keys
Lima (Peru)
London
Los Angeles / Downtown
Las Vegas
Louisville
Marseille
Martha's Vineyard
Memphis
Mérida (Mexico)
Mexico City

Miami & South Beach
Milwaukee
Myrtle Beach
Nantucket
Napa Valley
Naples & Marco Island
Nashville
New Orleans
New York / Brooklyn
Nee York / The Bronx
New York / Downtown
New York / Midtown
New York / Queens
New York / Upper East Side
New York / Upper West Side
Orlando & the Theme Parks
Palm Beach
Panama City (Fla.)
Paris
Pensacola
Philadelphia
Portland (Ore.)
Provincetown
Rio de Janeiro
San Francisco
San Juan
Santa Monica & Venice
Sarasota
Savannah
Seattle
Sonoma County
Tampa Bay
Venice (Calif.)
Washington, D.C.
West Hollywood & Hollywood

Made in the USA
Lexington, KY
30 April 2015